Words in Danger

Copyright © Lindley & Milazzo 2024
ISBN 978-0-913123-42-3

First published by Galileo Books in 2024
FREEGALILEO.COM

Cover art by Miwa Matreyek

Book design by Adam Robinson

A portion of book sales go to Water for People
WWW.WATERFORPEOPLE.ORG

[DEFINITIONS TO]
WORDS IN DANGER
[OF FALLING OUT OF THE VOCABULARY]

ERIC LINDLEY & JOE MILAZZO

GALILEO PRESS

Words

Bandage	57	O'clock	11
Boredom	67	Plough	52
Brace	48	Plural	69
China	35	Present	22
Community	3	Presume	42
Converse	17	Refresh	28
Cotton	44	Settlement	54
Couth	55	Snide	15
Dark	5	Stomach	60
Discern	65	Submission	9
Drain	31	Sure	46
Effort	76	Tie	61
Exodus	25	Touch	7
Favor	40	Trap	71
Freight	68	Viable	63
Friend	62	Visit	51
Glass	38	Wait	50
He	66	Well	70
Inch	26	Will	77
Laugh	75	Wolf	33
Mercy	19	Write	1
Music	73		

Write

v.

1 To make visible; to call into being.

> **AS IN** "I would have been older than you, but you were written first."
>
> **AS IN** "I would have been disjunctive, but for what, in that same hour, and plaintive, writes."
>
> **AS IN** "I would have been here on time, but amphetamines were written into my bloodstream, and everything was too beautiful to be wasted in disarray." as in "I've written desperation into my brother, and now his fingers can't untie themselves."
>
> **AS IN** "The diagnosis writes itself."

2 To stagger out of Edenic climes, and the Light of Hope you want so terribly to be scorching your back instead droops ahead of you in tepid disapproval, a dishrag sourness pressed into your eyes and nostrils no matter how piously you labor to shield your face with your uncovered hands. To cast a shadow.

> **AS IN** "The will is fixed in wandering; the carcass writes."

adv.

1 Insincerely. Without regard for consequence.

> **AS IN** "He spoke write at me. His words smelled different; they were seraphed."

adj.

    1 Realer-than-real. Like resuming an argument after a quick jog around the block.

        AS IN "It felt write to lay myself as flat on the floor of the tub as I could get myself, and let the water from the shower fall down. It's like I had written each droplet."

n.

    1 What something that has always existed is called in the act of pointing that thing out.

        AS IN "Each split-second's new you, each write, is a headstone to every previous you, dear writer, dear written."

Community

n.

1 A clean, white lasso. It has red strips at one end, circumscribing the cylinder of knit, marked like a talisman.

> AS IN "You're thirsty because you're afraid of your neighbors, and you grew up rich but your parents never let on."

> AS IN "The thin thing swinging above your head, or the thing you keep momentous while you jump in and out, the silly flop of leather fringe on your chaps bouncing like a long-haired show dog—it's from an earlier time: now they treat the systemic errors—the gaping horror of isolation, etc—like planned, satiable desires to be not-quite-taken-care-of. It's a stadium of people watching you jump in and out of a bright white lasso that you are keeping elliptic. It's a stadium of people with mirror neurons, jumping out of their skin."

> AS IN "Remember, the sky is a circle, like a circle also a blade, like a blade also turning, like turning also boredom."

adj.

1 A way to describe certain commercials.

> AS IN "The one where she discovers everything and shakes her head, and pulls out the box with the right emblem on it, and the scene wipes into perfection is very community. Her child comes back to life. She lives forever."

2 Possessed of an appetite for minor stings, slight nettlings, low-grade neuroses (i.e., anxieties made of fiction).

AS IN "A feverish community filled her mouth with sand. Suffocating somehow at the heart of all this sifting, she could feel it, a thrill horseradish-y and alien to the tooth. Native to the tongue, it was cultic. Its mystery's name was worship."

adv.

1. As if it were plucking the Great Web.

    AS IN "I avoided stepping on cracks, and apologized community to the stairs when I walked upon them."

v.

1. To make whole; to absorb into the godhead.

    AS IN "With enough sacrifice, you too will community."

2. To cobble or otherwise repair shoes.

    AS IN "Don't go sojourning communitied with proverbs, and little else."

Dark

v., chiefly intrans.

1 To utter a loud, harsh cry after filling one's lungs with reflected moonlight, the panic of moth wings, or some similarly poetic (i.e., identified with the penumbral) material.

>   AS IN "What if God should dark?"

2 To expectorate milkily.

>   AS IN "The drunkards dark."

3 To expire in manic convulsions, with one's laughter, shrill and attended by a sizable audience, exploding the essence out of halos as if they were yesterday's balloons.

>   AS IN "These two incommensurate ideals dark in a single body."

n.

1 What isn't able to be read.

Touch

adv.

1 At a great distance. As if by magic.

> **AS IN** "I communicated touch, and it was never enough." as in "Our technology operates touch." as in "And with that I ascend into the regions of the ice mountains and am lost touch."

adj.

1 Realer-than-real. Like talking to someone you love when you both have severe headaches.

> **AS IN** "The last five years have been inexplicably touch for me. Like, I finish work and suddenly I'm home, eating dinner, and suddenly I'm waking up again to go to work. There's lost time, but I can fill in every second in vivid detail, because the moments have been overlaid from day to day in such perfect mesh that the contrast and saturation really jump out. Even the way I peel the skin off my dinner roll and butter it before eating the fluffy, white center. I'm afraid of dying."

n.

1 A way to obscure information.

> **AS IN** "In the end we relied on touch, so society will be spared the grim truth."

2 A musical form, most commonly associated with peoples coping with not the actual historical consequences of their disenfranchisement, oppression or stigmatization, but rather the lingering consequences of the same, and generally featuring an eight-bar or twelve-bar structure that, using bent tones (typically at the first, fourth and fifth positions), moves from tonic, to the major second, to the minor third, to a fourth (from the tonic), to a fifth (from the minor third), to the major sixth and, finally, to the minor seventh. Or, any musical composition that, not being rooted in the authentic vernacular of the subcultural context described above, imitates this progression.

> **AS IN** "In that musky backwash of vibrato, we couldn't not know it: touch is responsible for the over-sophistication of our ears. Touch had cadenced our orations of our eyes."

v.

1 To placate with words or actions that are known to be untrue or at least hollow.

> **AS IN** "The nation was so tired of being sad that we banded together and touched one another until we could fall asleep."

Submission

n.

1 Euphemistically, a "procurer" or agent employed exclusively for the currying of goodwill and / or renumeration. Said agent is only awarded the status of a submission should he or (infrequently) she be successful at his or her task, appellation thus being retrospective and never a matter of direct address. I.e., the submission is never addresses as such, nor does he or she recognize him- or herself as a submission while serving in that role. Submissions are key figures in both national superstition and folklore, and stories of submissions who fail to suppress their self-consciousness in the execution of their duties have had a profound influence on our moral literature. Because "submission," strictly speaking, has no stable denotative—much less literal—meaning, and it may be argued that, by virtue of it currency being entirely reliant upon the specific and ephemeral circumstances of its each usage, the word is demotic proof of the theorem broached by Wittgenstein's in Remark 258 of the *Philosophical Investigations*.

[**NO EXAMPLE,** as in available.]

adj.

1 Not unwanted, but unenjoyed. Applied to the direct object of transitive verb phrases to imply that the thing was shed like persona, but willingly and without the threat of exposure or face-lessness.

AS IN "I threw the chasm my submission wrist."

>> **AS IN** "I gave my heart the submission pills, and went dancing."
>
> **AS IN** "Submission pity, or." (Common agrammatical fragment).

v.

> **1** To perform an act with due awareness to the honorific context of said act. The use of this word over the similar "submit" indicates the desire to express particular awareness of social rank.
>
> **AS IN** "I duly submission my timecard."

O'clock

adv.

1 Of, by, or according to an "old-timey" feeling.

> **AS IN** "A Sunday's supper, chiming o'clock."

2 Reminiscent of the limited dimensionality upon which the use of objects depends, that liminally studded flatness that shines like a knife's molybdenum flat.

3 Specifying "why?", "what for?", "which is which?", or inquiry into any state of affairs in which explanation is desperately desired and urgently requested, in loud and repeated articulations, but in which the only assurance is that all explanations will be withheld by knowledgeable entities and / or forces whose motivations are unmistakably vindictive if otherwise obscure.

> **AS IN** "We were in bed, lying one o'clock, awaiting the chiming of betrayal."

prep.

1 (Used to indicate this wild, straying off, the whole scene, at the conventional angle, a thing with a certain weight, for that matter, the opposite tendency, now holding its ears, as far as life, a pang that a billion people share, outward darting, that clause about the boundaries of common decency, the way they stand out, very high and very straight, though capable of talking, including treatments, his elegiac praise, with better prospects for health, again objects of scorn, a tiny emerging light, what you would have to abandon in crossing, pulling it a bit out of earshot, the latent eloquence of what they were doing, whatever that is, a world without coincidence, the humorless, secularized Puritan, by itself from forever, unable to look up, that was show business, and to have applied, the quitting bastard, be it in ink or pencil, jetting on a blue plume, which had both vagueness and a point, not a dog, the speech of a rustic, when served, this utterly restless stillness, who was destined to become equipped, this method for finding, the quaint remnants, which deterred no one, a first member, which accepts bad teeth, this brazenness, a saint in his vitrine, the violent emotion, the grandest pattern, the skyscrapers, armies, prisons, airs and all, unannounced, across the big room, a self-deprecating therapist, following the burglary, as satisfying the questions of "how much?" and "how many?", in nearly every way, well-heeled, as a livelihood or obligation, wonderful one, the machine, unfulfilled promises, who wouldn't let it move, a rather conservative estimate, this path of duty, the valley where she had passed, those wastes, for such services, as often in those days, apparently the first, a parrot for your shoulder, those years, the record he had worn out, the original thought, the plus and minus of it, waves gone with the bronzed one, islands lucid and afloat, where there was an oasis of hot water, a world on which he dined on fish and fresh fruits, only a month into his training.)

> **AS IN** "the wifebeaters hit the showers / the panties bombardier / relatively speaking / upwind [i.e., impending disaster] it's all / o'clock / lord kitchener's guns" (Ceerig, "the last of the diplomatic channels," 1922).

adj.

1 Bound by inheritance.

> **AS IN** "I was born as though waking half-way through life, endowed with every ability to think and even to know and to properly hate, but upon that early arousal was unable to control even my eyes from rolling back under their wet lids; my head lolled on a limp, pudgy mallow of a neck.

Growing up was an act of forgetting, more than I beleive it was for other children, whose joy in discovery made me more desperate than jealous.. Inconsolable, I practiced first blinking, then babbling, and standing, and hitting balls only with the perseverance of someone who was only tracing through their steps from earlier in the day to find their lost keys. I repeated actions I know I had done, so that in doing them again I might unlock the life I had truly built, and not this frail, o'clock pittance in which I found myself."

AS IN "You're not thinking. Your words are all o'clock before you've even thought of them."

2   Confined, as for a creative procedure.

AS IN "He first examined the page for imperfections against the natural lightbox of the sun. Upon seeing the flex of grit, or some other trace of inconsistency, chemical or physical, he circled it with the ink of a ball-point pen, and when all of these small spots—those visible to the naked eye—were duly check, clean and o'clock, he simply, put the page on the piano stand—where sheet music might go—and played sounds like blood oranges rotting."

Snide

adj.

1 It latches onto nouns like butter latches tinily onto the pitted face of toast.

> **AS IN** "Television is snide, because it better hides the difficulties of living." as in "I was sincere, but my cheeks got too red to control that other person's head with the palms of my hands—the fur on their ears fell out, and became too much like me." as in "The snideness is an easier transition when the camera is there, asking for noise that doesn't beg for attention—it wants us to pretend we have it begging, or something."

n.

1 It's a book that has sold well to boys who read to preserve a sense of themselves as readers. Or to make the fantasy of literacy, of currency passable.

> **AS IN** "The snide feels good in my fingers—it's like thousands of layers of latex house-paint."

2 the *élan vital*, superabundant with black suits, and it pays, just this once, to imagine a subway car as disgorging phallus, the hurry of fiduciary spores, a livid-going-on-lurid motility that won't be postponed, subterranean this much, much longer.

> **AS IN** "The snide, vegetal and animal alike, brings about, and in engendering, yields."

adv.

1 Obliquely. In-order-to-obscure-by-choosing-a-somewhat-more-honest-but-less-direct-answer.

> **AS IN** "I talk snide when you ask me how I am, because I've been away from home, working in the middle of a pyramid in the city. I tell you I want to end it—which is true—when I really just need a different job."

v.

1 Deflect.

> **AS IN** "I can snide the bullet that would kill me. Put the gun to my warm chest."

2 Make-safe

> **AS IN** "I can snide us to a bigger home, where no one can reach us."

3 To cause to waggle, undulate or waver in such a way that an otherwise potentially injurious phenomenon's (e.g., an arrow's) linear capacities turn particulate, granular, available to plucking or pinching(-off), the purchase of fingertips, esp. at their daintiest, cherries sprout to sunder the sclerosis of this shaft, this rod, this cudgel now efflorescing if not recrudescent

> **AS IN** telegrams, or "..."

Converse

v., intrans.

1 To labor in such a way as to make a livelihood out of what, under conventional circumstances, would be a leisure activity.

2 You don't know, or you don't say what that you know, or something aligned with a strong sense of sometimes, something inextricable from experience itself, intrudes upon and then murders saying, so all you can speak of is the endless tragedy of this, your cannot, you can't, your cant, your worship, you cast a shadow across everywhere, you shadow falls short of everything, you are a lever, you are a ladder, your face is a solar apostrophe: you and your you're.

n.

1 A well-worn association.

AS IN "She glittered, adorned with converse."

2 A gift of chance. Generally lacking social or economic currency, but endowing the witness with joy or a kind of disgust that is like scratching an itch.

3 Similar to (2.), but referring specifically to internet-distributed memes involving domestic animals performing perversely humorous acts of ingestion. A dog eating a mango. A bird with something that's just too big not to juggle.

adj.

1 How do we cope with the graft of our being founded on invention? how do we gentle reminders of our solipsism? how do we rescue the pattern of being from rapaciousness?

2 in the presence of a sound, orange or auburn, the names hee-ing, their hees set to hawing, and their hee-hees haw, and their haws hee-hee, etc.

3 I do not want to agree with this conclusion, but, serial and keyed-in, I find I must.

4 Not surprisingly.

Mercy

n.

1 Self-beyond-self, the subjectivity defined as (not by) an intense, paralyzing yearning, as of a socket for what would grind against its insufficiency in a joint.

2 Self-more-than-self, a vague prototype articulating in wands and runes and alembics this headlong imploring, "Please let it be me."

3 Self-in-excess-of-self, whatever is responsible for the disturbance you feel but cannot ascribe to any other agency, principle, or entity.

4 The self of the not-lover; the self that is the not-lover.

> **AS IN** "Strange celebrations came to me in my mercy."

adj.

1 Done with the high-minded narcissism of a god or parent.

> **AS IN** "A mercy killing."

2 Done secretly in the best interest of one's idea of oneself. Selfish, but in such a way that the agent of a mercy-event will die happily knowing that anything done was done in such a way that it appealed to some fictional, higher self. If the hands shake, they shake with holy resolve. If the eyes close, they do so to be closer to the world-soul.

> **AS IN** "If the mouth is dry and the teeth chatter, it's so the body can eat itself down to bone and then further, down to spirit: a mercy-chewing."

3 Done blandly, yet somehow skirting (with temporary hip dysplasia, or with a small hop) apathy.

> **AS IN** "I like my coffee like I like my reggae: sans mercy."

Present

adj.

1 There is and must be a likeness at the heart of unlikeness, that is, to be like or comparable in one's uniqueness; unlikeness as a measurable matter of degree rather than kind. You hear a woman's voice and you imagine you can imagine her body from that voice. Dream its conjuring, even, sleeping selves plotting the wreckage of their conscious hours. In truth, she is cloaked inside her mouth. A grandmother's housecoat, pastel and slung, with elephants for pockets. Shall I record in this log how her voice has traveled so far across a space in which our thoughts, her and mine, never knew one another but in which I've grown accustomed to her? Shall I sing of her to her? Shall I figure a heavy creaminess, a roll and gulp of upper arms, curves in the interstices, the intervals between the syllables of footfalls, mist, a summer's day, a rose, intemperate, champagne, cello, you, never another? Never another you?w

2 Of mixed ancestry; hybridized. The term carries no pejorative connotations, depending, of course, on one's views re: the exotic.

> **AS IN** "And yet the Ghost of Christmas Present blessed his four-roomed house."

3 Private, but not so much in the sense of "confined to individual concern" or clandestine. Rather, private in the sense of untranslatable, that which cannot be circulated or metaphorized (not that this quality does not discourage attempts at the same). Dispossessed of the capacity to withstand the rough handling of actual transit. So inherently subjective as to be unknowable; so personal as to be alienating; so singular as to be uncharacteristic. Shut within the body by the body's handiwork, like the hammering cuckoo in his clock, or the daughter-cum-sister within the *matryoshka*.

> **AS IN** "This language also uses the absolute reality of the present pain to secure the truth of cultural / political position."

n.

1 A carcass. Flesh left unfinished (i.e., skeletal) by a lazy death. As in, "Look who left you a present."

2 In contract law, any party who has recently declared bankruptcy.

3 In contract law, the negotiations by which property status is conferred upon insolvent individuality so that the garments may be divided into lots, and risk openly courted.

adv.

1 Like water, or saying nothing.

> **AS IN** "Presently, we are hungry with a hunger from someone else's holy books. It is unquenchable. It's a fire that burns without burning and a torrent from the rocks that presses the cheek to the ground like the heel of a boot, but cannot drown you. Presently, our fascia is velcro so small it works like water, too."

conj.

1 A transitional word joining two phrases related paradigmatically but separated by great swaths of time.

> **AS IN** "Valkyrie once flew overhead, present drones crowd out the sun and stars, exodus their souls collect in some white tower with those of the dead."

2 In between, but only under circumstances in which two distinct entities (or qualities) cleave to their likeness; in between-ness when and where there is no room (or capacity) for intrusion, intervention, the encroachment of an em dash or underscore.

Exodus

v.

1 To aspire to a conventional sort of virtuosity.

2 To fancify one's language and / or conversation, and in the service of one's own dickishness.

3 To cloak with a contronym.

4 To troll while pretending to prophesy, or vice versa. This is why we recommend the use of a PO box for all mail order commerce. Behind that paywall, a bathroom with a push-button lock, a keyhole plugged with the same cotton balls used for self-frottage, an egg beater, the hot broth of narrowcast outrage.

conj.

1 A transitional word generally following two phrases that are metaphorically linked, albeit with one prominent exception, which itself typically follows this word.

> **AS IN** "My mother squeezed out water with her hands, present there were once machines to do it better; exodus, it mattered then to do it better than a human could."

2 A less common variation: a transitional word generally following two phrases that are metaphorically linked, albeit with a commonly accepted exception that the speaker intends to question in this particular usage. Associated with archaic plays and conservative newspapers.

Inch

n.

1 Let's talk baseball. Let's talk the atomics of the game. Let's talk the game itself, outside the boundaries of its rules: the spectatorship following whitely, the fields shit-green, shit-verdant, the lines of its reaches and conservations. Baseball is for talking, not diagramming. Talking is sport, for in talking about what we saw maybe we see it better than we did. I know what I saw, and what I saw I cannot look at again, not for another season or two. A bad jump, or a jump misplayed, a chance with lost outlines in the lights, foreground slapping against background with a rubbery intensity. To win you need to cultivate a certain blindness. You win running on a fuel of blindness, all vision pulled down to a single dot by great gulpings of air that tastes both milky-thick and like liniment burning. This is why you smear your uniformed self acrid. The ball is coming, the ball is going, past mere distance into measure (that's the cracking you hear, objects emerging from probability, spin, into statistics, where they settled or stop rolling, gloved or not). We have to talk baseball to save it, glare by glare, from the incessant streaming of its own adjustments. Praying hands decline only to trebuchet back into a painfully parallel ecstasy. Wands worry. Soft vaults of caps grease themselves with tilt. The ballast of manhood is baby-like, moved after habit in cradles, protected out of the way; you keep it from particular exertions. Look, and repeat, for any narrative whose outcome depends upon a bouncy physics will always invoke a cosmology.

2 The evacuated circus resembles what they used to call a "computer game," wherein computer is not a platform on which to play, a medium, so much as a process, i.e., a game resulting from advanced computations, a game rigged by the certainties of math. Numbers with a finite number of divisions dividing themselves—warning arrows fired by a hidden archer—from each other.

3 This is what it must feel like to be the hammer that, in Thomist cliches, is caused to fall. This is how iron must subjugate iron, leaving it blunt and lusterless.

Refresh

v., trans.

1 To share; to offer a helping of something not necessarily desired because it is generally accepted to be of questionable if not limited utility or value.

2 To consume any delicacy unknowingly or in an unfeeling, disinterested manner. When used ironically—that is, predominantly—to eat one's heart out unconsciously, as if one were under no compunction (i.e., had not been taunted into the act) to eat one's heart out yet proceeds to eat one's heart out all the same. As in, "With these sweet thoughts do even I refresh my labors, even as such sweet relieving itself, thought-out, is refreshed."

v., intrans.

1 What if reality is all tile-work?

2 What if everything is grid, or perpendiculars all the way down?

3 Do you fear the ascendancy of certain Asian economies? Are you afraid of the derivations suggested by a toothbrush reclining, turning clean under the greys of running water?

4 When all it is is facile. When all it is is pastiche. When all it is is saying "Shut up and deal." When all it is is pink hurtle and effervescent medicine.

n.

1 The now-and-then moment of waking, the terror, and the regarding of the terror

AS IN "Every night when I was nine years old, and then once a week, once a month, and a blip and stutter like that every few years. At some point the whole routine skipped a decade, and the feeling was different when it came back. The tracking was off, so I could see the black border around each frame, reach up through that border like Fritz the Cat and grab my own ankles, drag myself frame by frame into the future. A ladder of selves slipping through a ladder of acetate."

2   Also every other moment, the ones you viable.

Drain

v., aux

1 You get it; your arms, even, know the dance. It's so ingrained that the hoop they form looks good even in the shadow-scraped stucco walls of a southern dwelling. You dance like electrons pulled through the conduits of addiction—a horrible and boring Catherine wheel of habit in the frontal lobe: this is familiar pain. This is the look I give myself in the mirror when I'm crying and snap out of humanness for just an instant. A smile filled with snot. I drain slit the ceiling for the mice to fall through.

2 You wake up seated at the head of a table, and are asked to teach. This happens so often that you find yourself teaching again when you are asleep. You meet yourself as a child and teach her to undo her stitch in time. She does, and something gasps in your chest, but you can only teach to the nearest railing until she has completely done whatever she will do. You teach the sweat back into your scalp, knot your tie tightly, and put each loose foot in front of the planted one.

3 You wrinkle in proleptic forbiddenness. What was once food has turned predator, tentacled with "no"s. Don't think bread isn't post-post-colonial. You encounter yourself wizened and try and learn from your own archaeology how to splice the baby-talk back into the baby-doll. Its takes baking shovelfuls, worse than gravel. HIstory isn't time, it is time's catabolysis.

v., intrans.

1 To be read.

AS IN "When I set up shop here I just wanted a place for people to come who loved books and might want to talk to one another while they sipped coffee that my wife makes and thumbed through the things that I had found at times in my life that just might be meaningful in some if not the same way to them. But as the novels drained, I drained too, and found that youth wasn't wasted on the young so much as the living."

2 To be given the solemn ceremonies associated with burial but to be left afloat, on either air or water, for an indeterminate span of time. Akin to being marooned or stranded, but with the additional connotation of "for reasons morally fictive." As in, "I like me liking you. Don't drain me; like my liking just as much. Let me be your sickly student."

Wolf

n.

1 The rope in your chest that time pulls so slowly it tickles on the way out.

2 That water always flows downhill until it's heat.

3 Any automaton. The mechanism creaks along, its parts soft. Metal strips must be procured, their conductivity rounded, their corners fore and aft arced to that the rear teeth become a tickle. The tongue, a crone. Next, a cotton reed to pretend the spine is a soul. (Remember: soft parts.) The whole thing is bound up in its own free ends. As soon as it is swallowed, the contrivance respires itself (remember: flames, like soft parts, glutton on oxygen) back into position and you hear how you speak commands to it: in the swishing, panic accents of the murderer.

adj.

1 Knowing without seeing or experiencing. Knowing by guessing confidently and persuading away the errors.

> **AS IN** "If we are to survive the winter, we will need a wolf thermometer—something that tells us what should happen more than what is or what will."

> **AS IN** "The markers here are all off. What they did is wind tape around giant wheels of plastic—a mile long when you unrolled them, which they did, then rolled them up again. They did this along every road in the country, then the world, and put markers down each time. But what they didn't count on was the tape they used. It was pure wolf, if you ask me. And there's no going back: you and feel the teeth at the nape of your neck when you drive anywhere

late at night, and the accordion of time just pushing air so you know how closed the system is. If you ask me,"

AS IN that old joke, "Lemonade, anyone?" The wolf ones decline, lemonade—however iced—always being boiled, thirst being pure eagerness.

China

n.

1 Something with propulsion beyond itself, like a planet careening toward its twin.

2 Something made desirable by its own fragility.

> **AS IN** "What I dreaded most was separating everything we'd accumulated together over the years. These objects acquired in dumb hope, now corrupting them. Methodically. Touching each one. The towels, the china—which, if I'm honest, even in the best of times was haunted by its certain breaking. I'd absently drum an edge with my fingernail and at once imagine some accidental shattering, my feet bleeding from a stray shard months later. Dust in the wound. Little drops of blood from the den to the kitchen, all imagined, all baked into the cold lip of the saucer."

adv.

1 Indicating the area in which one is to swim, swim understood primarily in terms of its sunken aspect, not buoyancy per se; swimming as submersion, or an expression of "into," but scrubbed of abstraction, no longer a conceptual entity—i.e., text—but a (potentially disorienting) physical experience of dimensionality.

2 Activating going. Making going go. As in, "If you want to maximize China right now you might be better off waiting to see just how cheap stocks fall as other investors gradually begin to apprehend just how unbalanced the global economy really is."

3 In the manner of the circumstantial, and to the degree that place is misplaced, cause uncouples from effect, and time's bloodhound senses dull and antecedence and repercussion lapse, motive smouldering like a pile, tidy rather than vast, of burning money.

4 You don't have to like it. You can love it while leaving it. If things were still normal, we'd call pride proud. So keep kneading until the corn is as high as whatever animal makes its way back home.

Glass

adv.

1 I'm sorry, I forgot the words. That is, I'm certain there is something to be said that is nimble as it is horrible, and that the saying it plays Simon on the lobes, or a Zeldic Pattern-Of-Unlocking. But maybe a year ago I stopped looking. I think I was either happy, or distracted by fear, and i stopped looking. Sure, the realfear gripped me when i tried to sleep, or the passion caught me when I was sometimes able to sit with a pen or a guitar, but largely I forgot that I must be looking for The Pattern, and so I settled into television and the pleasure of touch and habit, and lost myself to whatever thrills come with jealousy or overshooting jealousy with grand articulation, and the darkness—or whatever we can agree to call the horror of what approaches when your back is turned—I forgot about it.

2 It's only now, and I hope this isn't too plain or too silly to just hear up front like this, but it's only now, with a sheet of paper and the compulsion to cover it before I am allowed to go to bed that I can say this. As much as I would like to track the steaming paw-prints of the horror and go back to the full-body shudders and freezings of terror, because there was a cachet or a specialness to that proximity, as much as I would like to track the beast back to the cave in the base of my spine, and wrestle something of sinew and teeth and know that my fingers would slip through sheets of fascia, and poke through comic lattices of spit and the world would be shiny with transparent fear and knowing. As much as I would like that, I think I may have forgotten how to fear that deeply, because it's no longer new.

3 A repetition without words, for the sake of measuring time.

4 A space carved out for threading one's fingers through one another, until the webbing is taut and crisp as a sail.

5 A laugh like an artifact.

v.

1 To over-extract your company's coffee via a rolling boil or stovetop percolation. What do you mean, you don't worry yourself? You know how terrible his jokes about what you serve. After-dinner is not before-bedtime, not entirely. There's the time you take, and the time taken from you on your behalf. The carafe is cracked along an axis of half-full. The neighbor's mister tips his cup for seconds, awful seconds you are pleased never to have.

n.

1 The file-folder, blued generic and vanishingly burst.

2 The files, collated by rainbow mutings and accordant with descension.

3 The file clerk, he is a he, parthenogenic like that, orthopedic on one towering shoe, and as thudding as obsolescence (meaning: his fertility depends upon the donations of his clones).

4 There are so many bands named "Dust," practically one for every genre. My favorite being the one you've never heard.

Favor

n.

1 X, and the whole world Xs with you.

2 Everyone is a bard, everyone being that him or her in love with the whole sad world, the world whose wholeness coheres by virtue of its sadness, provided they only have to sing along with and not sing that saddest of songs: the whole world, fully discovered and yet unknown.

> **AS IN** "The whole world is a revolution that does me no favors."

3 A colloquial unit of measurement. Technically, pseudo-scientific. You're having a conversation (remember those?), and the moment calls for some reference to the notion of scientific quantification. You want to wish that there were some way to pin down the precise feeling of overheating soldering your lap to the computer desktop on your groin. You want to have faith in fathering, but information is nuking your motility. You want to say carbon takes but a single form, and that it isn't anthropomorphic, demographic, or psychographic. But you'll have to wait; I'm looking up how quickly I can debunk you on my phone.

4   I I7 IV iv I III vi IV V I iv I :|

> **AS IN** "A suitor came one day to see mama, his hat in one hand and a ribbon-wrapped box of chocolates in the other. He sang to her of precious metals, foxes, and fighting, but there weren't enough violins in the world to melt her glacial heart. Not with us to take care of did she need another child of sorts, with stars in its eyes and hunger in its belly. When he could see that this nightingale act of his was of no use, he unraveled two great silver wings

and whoosh, just like that up the chimney. It wasn't five minutes later that we saw him right across the street. His kneeling silhouette in the living room window of Ms. So-and-so, puffing and collapsing like the blood red bellows of a frigatebird."

Presume

v.

1 To avoid engagement. To parry.

> **AS IN** "I presume you will want a warm drink when you come in from the cold. Put on your slippers. Coat your cough in hot honey, and dream of running over pin-pricks till it's time to work again."
> as in "I presumed the disaster until it was my children's thing."

> **AS IN** "The problem with politics presumes that politics are all obvious, even when their subjects are consistently occluded."

2 Rising, dawning, cresting, and thus to implicate, and primarily via an initial aspect both glorious and effulgent, the preordained and hypotrochoidal artery of one's transience.

3 However much you try and magnify death, it persists as a speck.

4 To unite in departing or the act of departing. As in, "Presumed behind."

5 To have read too few or too many books, either in life or on vacation.

> **AS IN** "Last year I showed up in Barcelona with a suitcase full of DeLillo and not a single change of socks. On day 3 the placard must have fallen off the handle because a maid kindly shook me awake and helped call my family. 'Do you have any idea what time it is?' I groggily sneered. 'Do you??' and for several seconds, before I fell asleep again, I heard this faint ingressive twittering. Either laughing or crying."

Cotton

v., trans.

1 To ellide, to tacitly embrace by ignoring.

　　AS IN "I cotton to anything with a little breath in it."

2 *Pejorative.* Of a short story set in academia, or dealing with the tribulations of being an academic, particularly one who harbors artistic ambitions and/or struggles to untie the apron strings of serial monogamy.

n.

1 Sometimes the process gets hung up with no time remaining. You watch as "0 seconds" dilates past designation, assumes dimensions that might be filled, packed even, with another kind of time. Time edged like a city. Copenhagen time; time submerged in the Scandinavian metro, dark in a way different from their winters. Sunsets like salmon filets. Bookless DMV time. Do you observe a form before you begin filling it out? The problem is you don't. You won't allow that much time. Such time being indecisive, irresolute, obedient in its assumed willfulness. (I don't want poetry that feels. But, then again, I want something more that poetry's weak philosophy; it's watered-down vinegar.) For minutes there are 0 seconds, no more, more than less, less than numb. 0 seconds as a finger hovers over an escaping keystroke. 0 seconds in which an output may still be aborted. What was it you were trying to accomplish anyway? How do you defeat productivity's heliographic duplication? How do you plat? How do you ungerrymader the Oversoul? Lavished with ancillaries. Ostinatoing away like Stephen Fry before having all the answers telepromted out for him gave him a nervous breakdown. Knob up on the woop, dial down the pew-pew. For years and years, the jacket disincentivized my ever spinning the LP inside. The sight of advertising is the sound of air conditioning. What rends rendering? 0 seconds fly by, like the fun that had to happen every time.

Sure

adv.

1 Expressing desire beyond the comprehension of the speaker.

> **AS IN** "Surely we can squeeze out another generation before heat death."

2 When weaving is unwoven, the threads make a ripping sound. It's not that they've forgotten friction. They've just fallen prey to assumption. Friction can be enclosed, but it won't be housebroken.

v.

1 The deepest comfort is in the thing or its opposite. That each sucking in has a blowing out, that I will duck to avoid the lintel again tomorrow, like I do every day, because my body has grown bigger in the years I have been alive, but will grow smaller again, and brittle, and soggy, and the things inside me that helped to eat my food will come to eat me, too.

2 All of this whispered to immunity's espionage.

3 All of this is screamed into a vase.

4 This is screamed into a pillow.

5 This is screamed into an ear: a human's ear.

> **AS IN** "We won the west, eventually. It took breaking the arms of the land with metal pliers the size of a horse. We broke the land's arms, then we broke its teeth out, straight out of its gummy little jaw, which is fine. In the sockets we planted cacti and urchins, because the land doesn't know

the difference, and it sends a shiver down our spines so we get tired enough to go to sleep after all the shivering."

AS IN "What is more discreet: shuffling through the room with the head down, or giving a tight nod to the occupants as you pass? There are books of etiquette on the topic—the etiquettes were tracked and cut with kosher knives before their skins were pasted in the book, and I think the colors are held fast with formaldehyde or some cousin. Would you like to see? Would you like to run your hand across the rippled surface of the Book of Nodding?"

Brace

adj.

1 With no other place to be. Poised on the lip of a cliff that is also a weak chin.

> **AS IN** "Something deeply shifted, but we knew still that we were brace."

2 With no place to be. Like being "at" work, or occupied by it. (Economics as demonic possession; the resume as the palest of pale riders.) Activity isn't a location, conditions don't have fabric-covered walls where you can unintentionally crucify images of your spouse/pet/loved ones. Disappear into coordinates in order to go past going, but don't sign off on this as if it were an imperative.

3 Old mister Granier seemed scary, but he wasn't so tough after all. That summer we learned everything about death and friendship. Being young is about a terror that reaches beyond mere intrudership. Or it is a spiritual intrudership. That summer we learned a lot, and I got afraid of myself instead of being afraid of everyone else so much. That summer I learned that I was just a blip in someone else's calendar. That was a big year, and in the end I learned a lot about myself, but that knowledge is like a wet bar of soap. That knowledge is like pure molten lead and my hands are tissue. The knowledge is a wet bar of soap and I am Don Knotts.

4 I'll tell you what that knowledge is: you can hear the banjo plucked slowly if you get close enough.

5 I'll tell you what knowledge isn't: chewing. Also: tanning. Also: *zapote*.

6 I'll Miranda before I Cassandra. I'll take center stage and cut down the nets.

7 I'll whisper it into the orange glowing flesh of your ear: you won't live to the singularity, because you were born too late in time.

> **AS IN** "We've run the tests, and everything is brace, ma'am."

Wait

n.

    1 Decrementing.

    2 It is very true.

    3 Read it fast, or not at all.

    4 Repeat.

    5 You can no longer get away with it.

adj.

    1 Pertaining to something experienced either mindlessly or without necessity. "The soda in my stomach is heavy and wait."

Visit

v. intrans

1 To, for all intents and purposes, erase oneself from a moment or several consecutive moments of interaction with a person or thing. To stare blankly but surely into the eyes of life, with still no spark looking out. Frankly, it's eerie, but not unexpected, and the erasure, when practiced, may also be accompanied by chatter inherited or osmosized from one's developmental ambience.

> **AS IN** "Nice weather we had long ago, eh?"

> **AS IN** "It takes all kinds. I keep a list of the kinds in the curling ladders of DNA in my arm. Most of them are unpronounceable, or have impossible grammars, but there are some that bring you casserole at the summits of personal, quotidian horror."

> **AS IN** "I have no preference, or prefer not to express any."

> **AS IN** "It must be Sunday evening; your grandmother is on the phone."

2 Ctrl+Zed; Ctrl+Naught; Ctrl+Thorn.

3 To sort, and totally nail it.

Plough

prep.

    1 "Not below, or through, but plough the skin there is the sensation of cold, rushing oil. Whenever it says your name."

    2 They told us freedom wasn't free. As it turns out, neither is prosperity.

Settlement

n.

1 The lucky clouds that eddy in projector-light.

2 A case of mistaken metonymy. Like beckoning entry through a door while stopping a doorway, or saying "as if" as if you meant to indicate when. That is, misprision which has the effect of turning a signified inside-out.

3 We dare no longer call them a captive audience. This poses a grave risk to brand safety. That said, we need to convey the degree to which they are happily defenseless, receptive to your messaging. They are digesting funnel cake, or queuing for a chance to be sick on a sponsored drop tower. Hit them with acronyms; heal them with casual game whose midroll is unskippable.

4 Graying at the sideburns is an index of the lapses in judgement to come. This is how you end up with a child who nicknames themselves Pontius. A daughter who calls you "daddy without irony."

5 Baptismal phlegm.

Couth

n.

1 Sharp, sharp teeth.

2 The specific procrastination inspired by book reviews.

3 The museum of the living.

> **AS IN** "The blues aren't cyan enough, but a little couth correction should take care of that."
>
> **AS IN** "Anonymous in the uncouth."

adj.

1 (*archaic*) Blunted or bruised.

2 Like the accordion folds in paper lanterns that will never be set aglow.

3 Like the scallops in a seashell bathroom sink (Corium, not granite.)

> **AS IN** "A human body in no way resembles one conceived for ravenousness; it hath no eagle's talon, no piercing sting, no cleaving of jaw, no such strength of stomach or heat of digestion as can be sufficient to convert or sublimate such freighted and fleshy fare. But if you will contend that you were born to an inclination to such food as you have now a mind to eat, do you then yourself kill what you would eat? But do it yourself, without the aid of implement or malice, as foxes, dragons, and leopards do, who kill and eat with one mind. Stalk an ox with thy teeth, worry a piglet with thy mouth, tear a lamb or a squealing thing in pieces, and pounce upon it and rend it alive as they do. But if thou had rather stay until what thou eat is to become dead, and if thou art loath to evict a

soul from its body, why then dost thou against nature eat an animate thing? There is nobody that is willing to eat even lifelessness even it alarms the gut's unfailing sense of where the carcass lies; so they boil it, and roast it, and impregnate it with fire and medicines, quenching and euphemizing the slaughter with menu after menu of sweet sauces, that the palate being thereby outwitted may admit of such couth." (Minoan epitaph, Knossos, 15th century BCE.)

Bandage

n.

1 I walk by choice. The shirtless youth, kouros with a mouth surlied by a Blow-Pop, doesn't have any poise that's not subject to destination. (Years before, these men, anyone of whom could be that boy's father, these men from the bakery would come in to the grocery store where I was promoted to cashier, about an hour before everyone else would be going to dinner, bouffants even more white from the enriched flour of their long shifts, and buy Blow-Pops by the pair. Maybe a pack of Newport Lights as well. But Blow-Pops, grape and strawberry. I'd watch them walk back across the highway, back toward the big warehouses of humidity into which they reliably disappeared from the surrounding neighborhood, the cardboard sticks of the suckers wagging out the punchlines to jokes I'd never be inside enough to see just how smashed their blacked-out windows really were.) Oh, ooh, ah: another sunny day. The man whose tattoos have turned blue under his laborer's tan, driver's side flung open to the Home Depot parking lot, asleep with his elbow on the wheel. I close my trunk unthinkingly, as I always do, a slam that transmits the meaningfulness of my convenience. This might be what wakes him. He looks awoken, I mean, unsure of the mise-en-scene perception is serving him (but certain he is perceiving), eyes less dazed than vulnerable, maybe even kind. This look isn't for me. It isn't for anyone. But, for as long as I am willing to pretend it doesn't happen that I am looking at him, or acknowledge seeing him in this, the moment of his most honest, interrupted consciousness—this look is my privilege. Slurpee cups and Blow-Pop wrappers and envelopes bearing the city seal (or is it just a logo) on the floorboards of his car. I'm not satisfied, and maybe it's that all thrills are cheap, but at least I get to drive away, and to my own exit music. While I'm popping my fingers to traffic, the doo-wop of summer bodes a dearth, promissory in a monotone.

v. intrans

1 Is it the protecting or the concealing that heals the most? Or is it something to do with moisture, that witless architect? Just a suitably damp bed for white tendrils of flesh to reach across the blood-slick void. Does it matter? The not-seeing at least makes possible that warp in time: the beginning, and suddenly the wound is forgotten, opened again, and forgotten.

Stomach

v.

1 What is it, in the throat, that parries each bite? If not energy, then what is released, exactly? A god that parrots love? A bruise with two arms, two legs, and a bruise? Five dazzling fingers that you could just bite the Dickens from, if you had your druthers, but you don't do you? Did you put your pants on one leg at a time, or did you cry for a spell and then wake up beside your love, with an armful of wet flowers and this everlasting grin?

2 When the smoke clears, it's not my lungs that burn, but rather the thought of infinite BURN that scares me from breathing. When I pass out, the ghost takes over, and boy am I glad?

3 They will make a machine for people like me, and it will even work the arms.

4 Colloquially, a volume of weeping. In the pathological sciences, a standard for quantifying the discrete amount of distress, sorrow, etc. eliminated in a single 60-second cycle of weeping. Also, a unit of measure useful for converting linear and spatial phenomena into temporal ones.

n.

1 You get used to it.

2 You're human.

3 You're welcome.

Tie

n.

1 They make them long enough, but not strong enough, as if by accident.

2 All the companies that might be are looking for someone like you.

3 An inbox strategy in which users create a unique folder to contain each new message. Often paired with a custom algorithm (based around natural-language keywords and simple Boolean valued-functions) that simultaneously classifies and archives each incoming message.

4 As if by design, they make them disintegrate, and into enough.

5 Studiousness. I.e., the descriptions enervate, blanch, sag like (but only like) bundles of slack capillaries. Their mythologies cannot rouse themselves from the obvious and all they mutter about is how much they'd welcome being swept away. Where their roots once held the line, appointees dream of crafting a fountain that perfectly mimics the mechanics of a stream… that is sweet water's very analog. But their dream is ignorant of the fact that, in certain civilized quarters, this is how widowers repent their outliving their widows.

v.

1 To tell a story with no end.

Friend

n.

1 I forget which motion of my fingers brings them into being: they've been soaking in sour alcohol, so they're white and sloughy, ragged, pulled off the bone. She tried to friend me but it burned. She tried to friend me but I became better and instead of speech, effluvium: platitudinous, rare, and meant wholly.

adj.

1 The sculpture is elusive: you can keep walking around and around, planetiously aching for the revelation just beyond the tangent of white stone—but of course it doesn't come. It teases you, the viewer; it tantalizes you. But when I say "ache", I am not speaking of the false ache of Tantalus, who could not ache because that is another people's word: who can't ache because he is a chalk enclosure. I mean *akanen*, I mean *ag-es*: the structural groaning of dread-want. *Ake*! It is a home on fire! "Ache" is just a house, painted red.

2 The breach, but only once it achieves a certain level of fame and can afford to dress its wounds with rainbows.

3 The bleach, penned.

Viable

v.

1 Take the two steps on denial's momentary journey. Write a confession in ink. Write over it in chalk, making another confession. Deny it sideways.

2 To prolapse, often to musical accompaniment.

3 The botched omelette lies bare, a surgery deadlocked in its own step-by-step incisions. It pays a weirdly demure tribute to the difficulties of teaching yourself, even if the subject is elementary harmony.

4 The intervallic bits line up, stair-step style. A proposal is sure to follow the path of the world's tallest escalator, as ridden (if that is indeed the right word) by the world's champion escalator rider.

5 To confuse a breathless proliferation of arpeggios for the incremental advancement of our inalienable rights.

Discern

v.

1 You want a souvenir so badly, but the degree of miniaturization that's been administered to the mascot, plaything or adult-world accouterment you'd otherwise never be separated from isn't enough to bring the thing into the scope of your affection, itself still in the pupal stage, i.e., territorial avarice. The souvenir isn't small enough to be cute or companionable. Somehow, it still possesses too much length, or breadth, or girth, and its proportions outline a false promise. You want something to cherish but it will love you back instead, and be rather unfair about it, too. Stranded between the manipulable and the awe-inspiring, this erstwhile (that is, unpurchased if not rejected) souvenir's self-control will impend over all else—a shadow with sun shivering around its edges and mind diligently erasing its transparencies, layer by layer.

2 That Cartesian trick: to vivisect the real, to lay it small and plain, piece by piece, and in so doing to conjure something better in your pocket. You can never take it out, but you do touch it now and then when the going gets rough.

He

n.

1 See **heat**, or **heat death**.

2 This word encapsulates my relationship to vitamin D, but only accidentally.

3 A temporary barrier fashioned from live butterflies.

v.

1 To shimmer with unsteady choreography.

2 Thus the miserable bell cow, pursued by anxiety. Thus the enslavement of of presupposing. Therefore we perform seven or eight different dowries.

3 Murmuring is dark like chocolate. Whispering is a law of attraction. Architecture owns a face, but only when unsunken, beached.

Boredom

pronoun, plural

1 Without a name. I don't mean a name never proffered, a name rescinded, expired, unavailable to recall. A name extant. But outside the serial parochialism of any name's lissome Erector Set, what? Numinousness measured in odd cents. A cheap thickness of room temperature, like bottled water. Enter the salted humidity as if it were a lesson you could deplete. I do so many things that are illegible to me. Leaving them undone would be better, for accomplishment snaps them off before they can lance another and leaves each root throbbing canine inside me. (Without: the shape a tongue twists into to nose out the masticated brands that mortar over a bite.) My midsection of spars. Moroccan blue is gold. Excluding a name is a spin of other name-like aggregations. I didn't want this nonoccurrence to be onomatopoetic. I didn't want to replace wanting with this coffee. I didn't assemble the parking of my car as a way to tell the world that now it could be called "morning." I didn't bring hot food back to my desk and ask myself, "Why Minecraft?"

Freight

v.

1 To inscribe, write or otherwise make marks that are to be read (more properly, read back) in non-linear fashion. To write a text that is both an Eulerian trail and a magic square.

2 To mumble from the heart.

3 To tabernacle under the umbels. To retire to the weeds to mildew the saccharine and honey the piquant. To waft and yet achieve something akin to harmony. If words could sing under their own sway, how they might.

n.

1 A term of venery for forgotten things. A freight of them, tugging or leaping phosphenic away from the center of gaze. How long is it now?

2 What was that?

3 I dreamed I was younger than the family dog, again.

4 It was doll-like, hot water bottle-ish, foiled in the guise of a fetish, an undergarment-esque membrane disclosing air via candied spectra. That is, an instant deflation free of the explosive.

Plural

adj.

1   The first breath of air was tacky in the lungs: barbecue sauce on jackfruit, or dirty fingers flipping pages. The paper "Yee-haws" against the eye's progress and how it tracks the brain's encasing.

2   No one planned the vacation, so its arrival has been more a grinding than a sweeping up. Glacial, if not massive. What version of us had gotten tickets on a plane, a hotel, the one nice dinner of the trip, the show, the tour of the palace? Where had we learned the kata for Walking by The River or Walking Downtown, and why did the terror only subside when it got too dark for obligation?

3   All the things you see that are a version of you.

Well

v.

1 Suffice. As in, sufficiency is only in the upward trend: the abundance that keeps growing.

2 It used to be that story was enough to patch the actual. But somehow story's ratcheting has lost its torque. Maybe I'd forced the handle to far against the mechanism hidden in its simplicity. Or its components took to meshing too well, each gear tooth a blunt star irradiating in the blood-dark of an assumed utility. Like today, how the pilot light capitulated to a green LED and the closet reached the limit of its caring. No longer would the coats mute its incessant roaring — not that any closet wants to roar, or cannot help but defend itself otherwise. So I flipped the orange breaker. It's switch was obese and, as it returned to its circuit-completing position, it made the sound of a diner's paper napkin scrubbing against a stubbly chin. My arms, unarmed. My feet without the comfort of a per capita. I phoned the police, but they had to leave as soon as they arrived, The lead detective determined that the pitch everywhere around us was mere days out of warranty. So I pursued the thread. I trimmed and capped the lines' fitful diameters. After the laundry's heat broke, I discovered one sleeve had kneaded its nylon and lining into a supple epoxy. By closing time, the remaining doughnut had filled its crookedness with a transparency of grease. "Call me Chuck," the emergency exit said.

Trap

adj.

1 Descriptor applied to objects in the dual, lesser world conceived in some religions. Maya, shadows on the cave wall. If you thread a fine enough path, past all the trap things, you've won. Sometimes you start at zero and can go negative, or get a point for each trap evasion. In this version, you start with all the points and keep losing them, Leaky Bucket.

2 Sentiment's motility is hallmarked by a certain sludgy quality.

3 To a superficial archaeologist, "1"s could be "I"s. Then the whole house of cards pulls off a ziggurat illusion. "Poof"s could be "boob"s.

4 Trick, or to be tricked.

Music

n.

1 An archaic form of waiting (see **wait**).

2 We are filling one wall of our den (itself beadboard-ed, satin finished, like a glaze of ice somehow to any slapping-on other than primer) with empty frames. Empty too of glass or its euphemisms, e.g., enlarged windows of nail polish, durable fractions of clear acrylic, the notion of exemplifying itself. But not of a certain granularity, resonances wound. Yet the thin lines and notchs haven't caused the anticipated X-rays to ooze free. The house's nerves inflame privately. We still have to listen for the stud-finder to protest. Such a monotonous old man, always complaining about the hats interfering with his view of the action, never outraged enough to complete the circuit from his finger to a stranger's shoulder and request a kind removal. If the light doesn't shift from green to red, does the pitch rise or fall? When we aren't looking to look — when we are only toying with the tokens of occupation, such as forks and checkbooks — we're slowly cognizant of a canvas both original and beyond. The opacity that is itself a frame. Shelves disappear into it; lampshades and security, too. We try and intervene with another hanging. Why not, if they are all gratuitous, all recursive, all primitive? (Remember: winding precedes folding. Flatness, like vocabulary, is acquired.) We measure from the corner or one mortise to the uterine feather of a distant tenon. Without realizing it, we've mastered grooming. Should we walk out that front door, we'll encounter not birds, not stones, not cars, not jobs, not the climate's scatterbrained bloodthirstiness. Only smiling parents so proud of us that they fail to feel the blearing of that one incisor foreshadowing a mudslide.

3 A replication that, while it may be perfectly functional and/or achieves its aim, nevertheless feels lacking.

adv.

1 Penury reaches around to the taut and nautiluses itself inside a ponytail.

2 You brought a plunger to an auger fight. Somehow, luck is still on your side. Until it folds up its podium, anyway.

Laugh

v.

1 To solve by erasing or enhancing. As in, "laughter is the best medicine."

2 To erase with tempera, gouache, or some other non-oil-based paint, with the aim of foiling a forger. As in, "Laughing academy."

n.

1 A swing made from a length of rope, a discarded piece of industrial equipment, a branch that can support the weight of no more than two thieves, and a confidence not strong enough to be classified as hope yet weaker than optimism.

2 A day did make a difference. Mr. Bones did slip on pie crusts. The metaphysical did ride a merry-go-round, heave, shake it off with instant wrists. A difference of a day salutes a roundabout.

3 A Joycean cheese.

Effort

n.

1 Blind or blinding effusion.

2 A contranym at the valences of pride and shame.

3 Where components may fail and there is imperfect information on whether a component has failed, then all honest components agree the faulty components do not collude together in an attempt to lure specialized fault injectors into a suboptimal strategy

4 Pshht.

Will

v.

1 Privileged hope, or hope with soft hands.

2 Soap is oil, sans sanctification. Even if sacred spaces echo, as this glossolalist froths, its micelles cant in vain, not even trashing or blurting. Each bathing tars us with poetry.

3 I keep failing up — faster than falling. They told me the terror in my chest was usable. You have to pull it gently, by wrapping it around something so it doesn't break (see **tapeworm** or **fishing reel**), but the metal strand of terror was actually useable when they got the whole thing out. (Tedium skeletonizes everything behind glass.) No terror any more — empty compulsion in its place. They made part of it into a paperweight — the terror — a clunky little clockwork I keep at my desk: blurry silver movement threaded over pulleys, depressing springs. Looks great on mahogany; matches my watch.

4 To count down. But you must keep your answers to yourself.

About the Authors

Joe Milazzo is the author of the novel *Crepuscule W/ Nellie*, two volumes of poetry—*The Habiliments* and *Of All Places In This Place Of All Places*—and several chapbooks. His work has appeared or will soon appear in *Black Warrior Review*, *BOMB*, *Denver Quarterly*, *Fence Full Stop*, *Puerto del Sol*, *Prelude*, and elsewhere. He is also the founder and editor of Surveyor Books. Joe lives and works in Dallas, TX. JOE-MILAZZO.COM

Eric Lindley is a musician, writer, and artist living in the bay area. His writing has appeared in *Fence*, *Joyland*, *Tammy*, and elsewhere, and other work at the Santa Monica Museum of Art, Machine Project, Telic Arts Exchange, The Knitting Factory, and The Smell. With Janice Lee and Joe Milazzo, he co-edited the online interdisciplinary arts journal *[out of nothing]* from 2009 to 2015. LIKEOVERFLOWING.COM

Miwa Matreyek is an animator, designer, and performer currently based in Vancouver BC. She is an Assistant Professor at Simon Fraser University in their School for the Contemporary Arts in the Theatre Production and Design area. She has been an internationally touring independent artist since 2010, and her work has been presented at the Sundance Film Festival as part of the New Frontiers section (2011, 2014, and 2020), MoMA, SFMoMA, Lincoln Center, REDCAT, The Walker Art Center, the Wexner Center for the Arts, and many more. MIWAMATREYEK.COM

www.ingramcontent.com/pod-product-compliance
Lightning Source LLC
Chambersburg PA
CBHW032048290426
44110CB00012B/1002